Dedicated To:
My students

Written By: Abigail Gartland

I was born around 300 in Rome.

I was a follower of Jesus my entire life.

I spent my days in deep prayer and thanksgiving for Jesus in my life.

One day as I was praying, I felt called to join the military in Rome.

I joined the Roman military and went to battle.

I knew that I was serving the Lord by doing my best, but I was so tired!

The Emperor, who was in charge of the army, did not like Christians.

He ordered that anyone who was Christian would be killed.

I was scared, but I was willing to endure anything for Jesus.

My life was sacrificed, but I went to Heaven to spend eternity with Jesus in 319.

Do you want to be more like me?

You can celebrate my feast day with me on February 7th.

I am the patron saint of soliders.

I pray for you every day of your life.

St. Theodore, pray for us!

pyright:

art: © PentoolPixie © LimeandKiwiDesigns
sed purchased: 1/10/2024

About the Author

Abigail Gartland

I love the saints and I love my faith. The idea for sharing the stories of the saints with little ones came when my dear friend were expecting their first baby. I wanted t create something as unique and special a our friendship. Each book is dedicated to very special people and groups who have enriched my faith in different ways. I am blessed to write these stories and appreciate the unending support of my family and friends. When I am not writing am a middle school teacher. I hope you enjoy these stories. I pray for each and every person who opens one of my books to learn more about the saints.

Abbie

www.ingramcontent.com/pod-product-compliance
Lightning Source LLC
LaVergne TN
LVHW050135080526
838201LV00120B/4913